W9-CKI-761

Fabulous FASHIONS of the 1980s

Felicia Lowenstein
NIVEN

Fabulous FASHIONS of the DECADES

Enslow Publishers, Inc.
40 Industrial Road
Box 398
Berkeley Heights, NJ 07922
USA

http://www.enslow.com

Library of Congress Cataloging-in-Publication Data

Niven, Felicia Lowenstein.
    Fabulous fashions of the 1980s / Felicia Lowenstein Niven.
       p. cm. — (Fabulous fashions of the decades)
    Fabulous fashions of the nineteen eighties
    Includes bibliographical references and index.
    Summary: "Discusses the fashions of the 1980s, including women's and men's clothing and hairstyles,
      accessories, trends and fads, and world events that influenced the fashion"—
      Provided by publisher.
    ISBN 978-0-7660-3554-6
      1. Fashion—History—20th century—Juvenile literature. 2. Fashion design—History—20th century—
Juvenile literature. 3. Lifestyle—History—20th century—Juvenile literature. 4. Nineteen eighties—
Juvenile literature. I. Title. II. Title: Fabulous fashions of the nineteen eighties.
    TT504.N582 2011
    746.9'2—dc22

                            2010010311

Paperback ISBN 978-1-59845-281-5

Printed in the United States of America

052011 Lake Book Manufacturing, Inc., Melrose Park, IL

10 9 8 7 6 5 4 3 2 1

Illustration Credits: © Aaron Spelling Prod./courtesy Everett Collection, p. 40; © ACE STOCK LIMITED/
Alamy, p. 12 (woman with spiky hair); Advertising Archive/courtesy Everett Collection, pp. 24, 35; AP Images,
p. 38; AP Images/PA, p. 42; AP Images/Reed Saxon, p. 17; courtesy Everett Collection, pp. 7 (Madonna), 28;
David Thorpe/Rex USA, courtesy Everett Collection, p. 41; © Embassy Pictures Corporation/courtesy Everett
Collection, p. 12 (Molly Ringwald); Getty Images Entertainment/Getty Images, p. 14; © iStockphoto.com/
visual7, p. 6; © King World Productions/courtesy Everett Collection, p. 15; Library of Congress, pp. 43–45;
© LondonPhotos/Alamy, p. 18; © MCA/Universal/courtesy Everett Collection, p. 22; MeyerPress/Rex USA/
courtesy Everett Collection, p. 34; © Mirrorpix/courtesy Everett Collection, pp. 1, 29, 30, 33; © Paramount/
courtesy Everett Collection, p. 4; © REGLAIN/Gamma/Eyedea/Everett Collection, p. 10; Shutterstock, pp. 8,
13, 19, 25, 26, 31, 36, 47; © Stephen J. Cannell Productions/courtesy Everett Collection, p. 7 (Johnny Depp);
© Universal Television/courtesy Everett Collection, p. 20; © Warner Bros./courtesy Everett Collection, p. 11;
William Hames, courtesy Everett Collection, p. 9.

Cover Illustration: © Mirrorpix/courtesy Everett Collection (woman in short black and gold skirt).

Contents

The 1980s

The 1980s

Something happens when she hears the music…
It's her freedom. It's her fire. It's her life.

Flashdance

What a feeling.

...ur passion and make it happen!

...PICTURES PRODUCTION · AN ADRIAN LYNE FILM · FLASHDANCE · JENNIFER BEALS · MICHAEL NOURI
...PRODUCERS—JON PETERS AND PETER GUBER · SCREENPLAY BY TOM HEDLEY AND JOE ESZTERHAS
...ON AND JERRY BRUCKHEIMER · DIRECTED BY ADRIAN LYNE · A PARAMOUNT PICTURE
...CASABLANCA RECORDS AND TAPES ▯◯▯ DOLBY STEREO · Copyright · MCMLXXXIII By Paramount Pictures Corporation.
All Rights Reserved

Jennifer Beals is featured on the poster for 1983's *Flashdance*. The movie was responsible for turning an ordinary, frumpy sweatshirt into a smoking hot fashion statement.

Wild and Crazy Fads

Beautiful young Alexandra Owens worked as a welder during the day. But at night, she danced at a club. The 1983 movie *Flashdance* told the romantic story of how she realized her dream—to be accepted to a major dance school. The surprise box-office hit also did much for fashion. The *Flashdance* styles became some major fads.

Played by actress Jennifer Beals, the lead character wore an oversized sweatshirt that was ripped. It showed off her bare shoulder. Women everywhere bought large sweatshirts and T-shirts. They ripped the collars and wore them proudly. The effect was that of a shirt slipping off the shoulder. It was a very sexy look.

Leg warmers were another popular fad from *Flashdance*. Similar to knitted socks that were open on top and on bottom, leg warmers were worn by dancers to keep legs from cramping. In the 1980s, they became fashionable outside the ballet studio and the gym.

Leg warmers came in all different colors and patterns. You could have found a pair that matched any outfit!

Women wore leg warmers with short skirts. They wore them over leggings. They even wore them over jeans. They scrunched them below the knee so the look was slouchy and casual. Leg warmers were everywhere in the 1980s.

So was underwear. It was even in places where you could see it! Women wore silky camisoles and lacey bodysuits as shirts under business suits. It made the suit look more feminine.

Pop star Madonna started wearing underwear as clothes during her performances. She wore lace corsets, close-fitting undergarments that shaped and supported the upper body. By the end of the decade, she was even wearing cone-shaped bras as tops onstage. Fans copied her look. It became well known in the 1980s.

Earrings were another popular look. Sure, women wore them, but so did men. Throughout history, men had worn earrings, but it was less common in modern times.

Introduction: Wild and Crazy Fads

In the 1980s, musicians and athletes started wearing a stud earring in one ear. Ordinary men started to do so, too. Some wore one earring. Some wore two or more. It became common to see men with earrings wearing everything from casual clothes to business suits. It was a way to express themselves. That's what the eighties were all about.

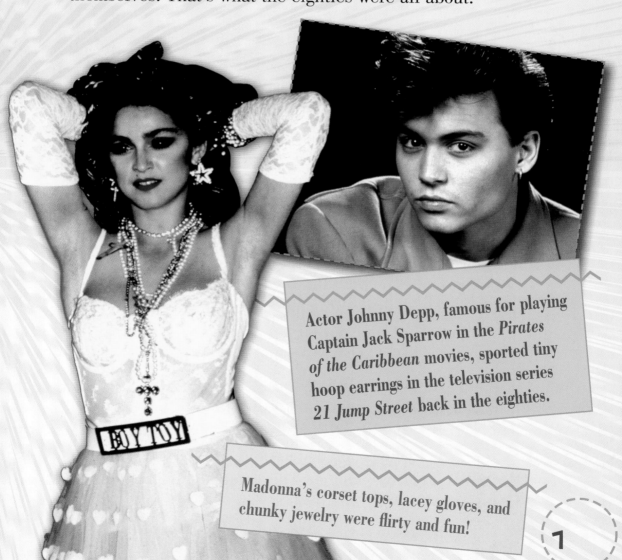

Actor Johnny Depp, famous for playing Captain Jack Sparrow in the *Pirates of the Caribbean* movies, sported tiny hoop earrings in the television series *21 Jump Street* back in the eighties.

Madonna's corset tops, lacey gloves, and chunky jewelry were flirty and fun!

Chapter 1

Hairstyles

There is one simple word to describe eighties hair—*big*. Even short hairdos were big. Women wore their hair high on their heads. They used styling gels and mousses to puff them out. There was a lot of hair during this decade!

It wasn't just women, either. Men styled their hair so it was big, too. It helped that there were blow-dryers. People could create their own big hairdos right at home.

Forget about hair pulled flat against your head. Women often wore big hair with bangs. Men wore big hair in different lengths, as in the mullet haircut.

Some people copied celebrities. For example, women styled their hair like the women on the TV shows *Dallas* or *Dynasty*. They copied the short blunt haircut of Great Britain's Princess Diana. They wore side ponytails like singers Debbie Gibson or Madonna.

Hairstyles

The popular rock band Poison and others like them were also known as "hair bands" because of their big hair!

It was definitely a dramatic time for hair. If you wore your hair the way they did back in the 1980s, you would be noticed.

Big and Curly

You can get your hair to puff out if you tease it. Teasing is combing back against the hair. It was one way that women created the 1980s' big hairstyles. They also used a lot of mousse and hair spray. It was not unusual for hair to stand several inches above the forehead.

American singer Tina Turner, wearing her hair in the typical big, poofy fashion of the decade, performs in concert in 1985.

It was also fashionable to have bangs along with big hair. Especially popular were curled bangs. Women would use a curling iron to create the look. You could wear curled bangs with straight or curly hair. If you didn't have naturally curly hair, you could always get a perm.

Make It a Mullet

The mullet was another popular hairstyle in the 1980s. It is where the hair on the top and sides is cut in short layers. The back is left long. Sometimes the change in length is smoothly blended. Other times, you can really see the two levels. Women and men wore the mullet. It was popular among famous athletes. Television stars and pop singers wore it, too. If you have ever seen Uncle Jesse on reruns of the TV show *Full House,* you would have seen the mullet he wore in the early days of the show.

Hairstyles

John Stamos's character on *Full House*, Jesse, was obsessive about his hair! His perfectly styled mullet stole the show in the early seasons.

So Purdey

The purdey was a popular short style. It was a blunt cut that was almost bowl shaped but angled along the sides to the nape of the neck. The bangs, and the rest of the hair, were all curled under. Princess Diana of England wore her hair in a version of the purdey. Her hair was parted on the side and swept back.

Actress Molly Ringwald wore a purdey on the sitcom *The Facts of Life*. She would later star in several successful films, including *The Breakfast Club*, *Pretty in Pink*, and *Sixteen Candles*.

An asymmetrical hairstyle definitely made a statement. This rebellious hairdo required a lot of gel and hair spray to get the one side of the head slicked back and the other side spiked up and over the eye.

Slide It to the Side

Women tried asymmetrical styles. That is where one side appeared different from the other. The side ponytail was part of this trend. It was popular with younger women in the 1980s. They pulled their hair to the side and put a rubber band or "scrunchie," a fabric-covered elastic tie, on it.

Chapter 2

Women's Styles and Fashion

It was time to get serious. That was the mood for fashion in the eighties. It was serious and businesslike. That's because it was the decade of the yuppie. That was the nickname given to the young urban professional. Yuppies were men and women in their twenties and thirties who worked in high-paying jobs in large cities.

The well-tailored executive was everywhere. That's because yuppies had money to spend on clothes. And more women were joining men in the workforce at the executive level. They were dressing the part, too.

Suits were popular for both men and women. Women also wore shift dresses, a classic style that had appeared decades before.

Four college girls model high-end casual wear also known as the "preppy" look. Preppy fashion could be considered the student version of yuppie fashion. Preppy students often became yuppies after graduating.

Fashion designers started creating clothes for yuppies. Department stores started showing designer sections, in addition to the skirt department or the coat area. This allowed stores to show off coordinated designer outfits.

Designers made everything from underwear to accessories. They even made dance wear and workout clothes. Yuppies had to have stylish clothes to sweat in, too.

Not everyone wanted to dress as a yuppie. Some young people went out of their way to dress very differently.

These were the punk rockers. It was a movement that started in London with students and other young people. It was a style designed to shock.

But whatever your style in the 1980s, one thing was clear. You had the freedom to express yourself. And your fashion did communicate a lot about who you were.

Dress for Success

The yuppie fashion was a powerful look. Women were working alongside men. Their outfits borrowed from the traditional male wardrobe.

Women wore tailored suits. Shoulder pads helped create wide shoulders, which mimicked men's shoulders. The jackets were paired with narrow skirts below the knee. Women also wore front-pleated pants.

Talk show host Oprah Winfrey embodies the yuppie look in her tailored suit with shoulder pads. She is one of the most powerful media personalities in the world, and she definitely dresses the part.

There were traces of femininity, however. Women softened suits with bow ties or scarves. They wore makeup and did their hair in soft feminine styles.

Return of the Shift

It wasn't all suits in the eighties, though. Women returned to a retro style known as the shift dress. It originated in the 1920s with the flappers and regained popularity in the 1960s. The shift was a sleeveless dress with a high collar that was cut straight down. It could come in various lengths but usually ended around the knee.

In the 1980s, the shift dress was popular in soft jersey knits. Women wore a shift over a shirt so it looked more like a jumper. On the popular TV shows *Dallas* and *Dynasty*, the women wore shift dresses in bright colors. These silk or polyester designs were in fuchsia pink, royal blue, and sea green.

Fashionably Fit

In the 1980s, fitness was big. It was a continuation of a trend that began a couple of decades earlier. Jogging had been popular in the 1960s and 1970s. Now there were also plenty of aerobics and dance studios. There were weight rooms and gyms. Americans were hooked on fitness as part of a healthy lifestyle. Of course, they had to have the fashions to match.

American actress Jane Fonda starred in many exercise videos in the eighties and early nineties. Those who wanted to be fit but didn't want to join a gym could work out right at home.

Lycra®, or spandex, was a popular fabric for workouts because it was light and breathable. It was stretchy and skintight. It showed every muscle and curve. It also came in bright colors and plenty of designer names.

Leg warmers and sweatbands completed the 1980s' workout look. Leg warmers were worn over the lower leg. Sweatbands were made of towel-like material. People wore them around their hairlines.

The Antifashion: Punk

Not everyone was a young professional. Some young people were part of the punk movement. This was an antifashion movement that was associated with a particular style of music called punk rock.

Punk rockers wore ripped jeans and T-shirts. They often sported multicolored hair. They might have had multiple piercings. Bright and sometimes mismatched clothing became their antifashion statement. Famous and everyday people alike embraced the punk look.

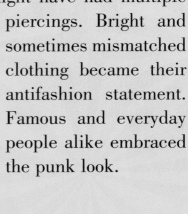

With her half-shaved head, multicolored hair, and unusual makeup, this girl is unmistakably punk!

Chapter 3

Men's Styles and Fashion

Women may have been dressing to look powerful. Men were dressing to look cool.

There was the *Miami Vice* look, a casual dress look inspired by the hit TV series of the same name. There was the "Thriller" look, which copied the styles on pop star Michael Jackson's music video "Thriller." There was the preppy look, named for the type of style found at a prep school. Then there was the designer sportswear look.

Suits have been worn for business throughout the twentieth century and are still popular now. But their styles have changed through the decades.

FABULOUS FASHIONS of the 1980s

In the 1980s, suit lapels became narrower. So did the neckties that men wore. Three-piece suits, or suits with vests, lost some popularity. Pinstripes were back in style but were narrower and less noticeable than in earlier decades. Button-down shirts were worn with suits for business and also for casual wear.

In general, the styles of the 1980s allowed men to have some fun with fashion. They could express their individual styles. And they certainly did!

Made in Miami

Miami Vice starred Don Johnson and Philip Michael Thomas as undercover detectives in Miami, Florida. The creators of the show used the pastels and bright colors associated with Miami Beach in both the scenes and the clothes.

Philip Michael Thomas (left) and Don Johnson look cool and confident in their *Miami Vice* ensembles!

They stayed away from anything red, beige, or brown. As a result, *Miami Vice* had a cool, casual look that could almost be described as tropical.

The clothes the actors wore had a distinctive style. They wore designer Italian blazers over pastel or white T-shirts. They wore white linen pants and loafers without socks. Ray-Ban sunglasses completed the look. The show was watched as much for the fashion as for the plots!

Fashion Thriller

When Michael Jackson released his album *Thriller*, it wasn't only the music that attracted attention. The fourteen-minute-long music video of the same name featured a werecat and zombies, and it caught America's eye. It had plenty of great dancing and style. It launched a whole new wave in men's fashion, particularly with young fashion-conscious men.

They loved the red leather jacket with its zippered details. They paired it with black or red leather pants and sunglasses. Some even wore Jackson's signature white sequined glove and copied his curly, gelled hairstyle, too. Even though they had been around for years, aviator glasses and stylish leather jackets, especially red ones, became associated with Michael Jackson.

A still from Michael Jackson's
"Thriller" music video.

Prepare to Be Preppy

Preppy is a term to describe a conservative style. It is a style popular at many prep schools attended by wealthy young men and women. The clothes are often designer, expensive, and monogrammed, or feature a design made up of letters that represent a person's name.

The preppy look includes polo shirts, argyle sweaters, blazers, and loafers. Colors are often bright. It is a neat look with a classic style. For example, you can put a preppy person from the eighties back in the thirties, and he or she would fit right in. As a matter of fact, the preppy look continues to be popular among the young and wealthy.

Parachute Pants

Think of the slick, slippery feel of a parachute. Now imagine that material made into pants. You have an idea of what it would be like to wear parachute pants.

Parachute pants were especially popular with fashion-conscious young men in the eighties who wanted to look a little less polished and a little more "street." The pants were tight and shiny. They were made for break-dancers. These were dancers who used acrobatics in their moves, often spinning upside down on their heads! The light and strong material stood up well. The pants would often have lots of zippers to add style.

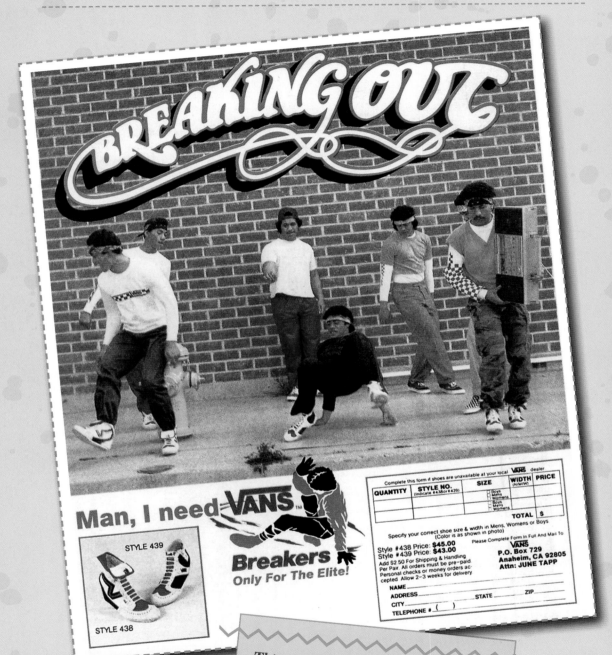

This ad for men's sneakers features break-dancers in parachute pants.

Chapter 4

Accessories

What people wore on their feet made a real fashion statement in the eighties. Yuppie women opted for classic black pumps at work. Both men and women wore designer sneakers for their workouts and for casual wear.

Dr. Martens boots, also known as Doc Martens or just Docs, originally were worn by punk rockers, following the antifashion movement. But the boots lost their wild image in the eighties. They became popular with young people who wanted to be fashionably dressed.

Footwear wasn't the only popular accessory. It was also fashionable to wear large, chunky costume jewelry, wristbands, and neon-colored sunglasses. It seemed the bigger or more colorful the accessory, the better. Women also wore fingerless lace gloves and tied lace scarves in their hair to add a touch of elegance and femininity.

Dr. Martens Boots

Dr. Klaus Maertens first made his comfortable walking boots in Germany in 1945. They had a special cushioned sole. The boots were so comfortable that policemen and postal workers wore them, even outside Germany, in England.

But the boots got a bad image when they were seen on the feet of violent gang members. They were also worn by members of the "skinhead" movement. These were young people who used violence against anyone who was not white.

By the 1980s, Doc Martens were worn by many different kinds of groups. They were worn by punk rockers, workingmen, and the police force. They were even worn by women with flower-print dresses. Because so many different people wore Doc Martens, they became less associated with one particular group.

Those who were fashion conscious and those who were antifashion both sported Doc Martens. The boots looked good with ripped jeans or flowery dresses!

Designer Sneakers

Remember those designer workout clothes? Well, there was plenty of footwear to go with those outfits.

Different styles of tennis and running shoes had come out in the seventies. By the eighties, there were lots of choices. There were different styles for tennis and basketball. There were aerobics shoes. These were brands like Adidas, Nike, Fila, Puma, and Reebok.

Some came up high on the ankle. These were known as high-top styles. The sneakers came in a variety of colors and trims. Some were more for fashion than they were for the gym.

Celebrities from sports stars to musicians had them on their feet. Rock stars Mick Jagger and David Bowie wore them in the "Dancing in the Street" music video. Whether one was watching TV or walking down the street, designer sneakers were a familiar sight in the 1980s.

The Bigger, the Better

Costume jewelry had been popular throughout the twentieth century. It was affordable and could look just as nice as real jewelry. In the 1980s, that trend got bigger, literally.

Jewelry wasn't just an accessory in the eighties. It was a focal point. Sometimes jewelry was noticed more than the outfit. People wore large necklaces and chokers, supersized earrings, and big brooches or pins.

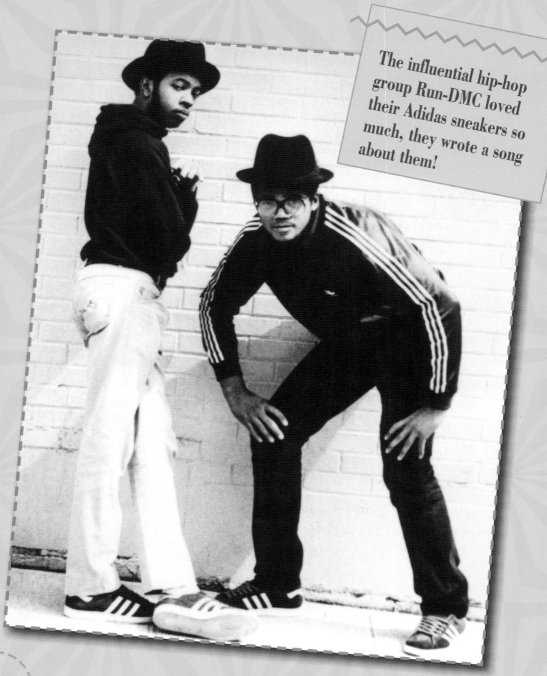

The influential hip-hop group Run-DMC loved their Adidas sneakers so much, they wrote a song about them!

Notice the huge pearls, bold brooch, and clunky earrings worn all at once! There was no such thing as accessorizing too much!

Lace and Fingerless

Cut off the fingers of your gloves, and you have a fashion statement. At least that's what happened in the 1980s. New Romantics and punk rockers alike wore the style.

But it really took off when celebrities embraced the trend. When pop star Madonna wore her lace fingerless gloves onstage, it was an immediate hit. Rock star Billy Idol also wore a leather version of them. They were a definite "dress-up" accessory and not at all like ordinary gloves that are worn for warmth.

Pop singer Cyndi Lauper accessorized her flamboyant outfits with lace fingerless gloves.

Chapter 5

Fads and Trends

Say "stirrup pants," and you're probably thinking of a style in the 1980s. That is because stirrup pants were popular during this decade. So were cowl necks and bat-wing sleeves. In fact, the eighties had its share of fads and trends. They might not be as popular as they once were, but if you look closely, you might even spot some of the eighties wear on the streets today.

Suits "On the Run"

You might expect women to wear heels with business suits. But in the eighties, plenty of women also wore sneakers!

In 1980, there was a transit strike in New York City. The trains and buses stopped running. It was a long walk to work. So women wore sneakers with their suits and changed into regular shoes when they got to their jobs.

The trend did not end with the transit strike. The buses and trains were running, and the women were wearing their running shoes. It became a common sight in cities across America, and the trend continues today.

Not Just for Equestrians: Stirrup Pants

If you lived in the 1980s, you probably would have had at least one pair of stirrup pants. Stirrup pants were similar to the stretch pants worn a few decades earlier, in the sixties. They were made of a soft knit fabric. They became narrower near the ankle, where there was an elastic band that slipped around the foot. It held the pants in place.

Women wore stirrup pants with oversized sweaters and sometimes sweatshirts. The finishing touch was a flat shoe that showed off the stirrup.

Power Dressing: Shoulder Pads

Big shoulders were all the rage for women in the 1980s. Shoulder pads had appeared in past decades, such as the 1930s and 1940s. But they weren't as big or broad as they were during the eighties.

Shoulder pads were found in everything from business suits to evening wear. There were even detachable shoulder pads in knitwear, T-shirts, and sweatshirts. That way, women could decide if they wanted to wear them or not.

Stirrups are similar to modern leggings and serve the same purpose. Neon colors were very popular.

Because big shoulders were a bit masculine, designers softened looks by using silky or feminine fabrics. They also added jewels, lace, and other details. Women sometimes pushed their sleeves up to show off contrasting linings. It was a way of accessorizing the look.

Everything was big in the eighties—hair, jewelry, shoulder pads! This model still looks feminine in a giant padded blazer because she feminized it with dainty gloves and high heels.

Try Bat-wings on for Size!

Think of a bat spreading its wings. Now you have an idea of what bat-wing sleeves might look like. Also called a dolman sleeve, the bat-wing sleeve is long and loose. It is cut so it is very large at the armhole. The sleeve extends from waist to armpit. The effect is as if the wearer had bat wings.

The bat-wing sleeve was a classic look for the eighties. It was a style that could be seen on the streets of your town and on celebrities on TV.

These women soar high in the fashion world with their bat-wing-sleeved sweaters!

A Cable pattern for this crew-neck jumper by Tour de Force with beautiful batwing sleeves. Hand wash. See size chart. Fibre: acrylic. **Natural.**
YS 206 Jumper
Sizes 14, 16, 18 £19·99
20 wks £1·00
Sizes 20, 22, 24 £20·99
20 wks £1·05

B Lacy jumper by Honeysuckle has crew neck and batwing sleeves. Hand wash. See size chart. Fibre: acrylic. **Natural or black.**
YS 172 Jumper
Sizes 14, 16, 18 £17·99
20 wks 90p
Sizes 20, 22, 24 £18·99
20 wks 95p

C V-neck jumper from Jump has collar and long sleeves. Two pearl-type button fastening. Hand wash. See size chart. Fibre: acrylic. **Natural.**
YS 199 Jumper
Sizes 14, 16, 18 £17·99
20 wks 90p
Sizes 20, 22, 24 £18·99
20 wks 95p

D Button-through cardigan by Jump with lace collar. Long sleeves. Hand wash. See size chart. Fibre: acrylic. **Pink.**
YS 192 Cardigan
Sizes 14, 16, 18 £18·99
20 wks 95p
Sizes 20, 22, 24 £19·99
20 wks £1·00

E Pretty embroidery and delicate lace trims this jumper from Jump. Wide crew neckline and batwing sleeves. Hand wash. See size chart. Fibre: acrylic. **Natural.**
YS 185 Jumper
Sizes 14, 16, 18 £17·99
20 wks 90p
Sizes 20, 22, 24 £18·99
20 wks 95p

35

Chapter 6
Pop Culture

In the 1980s, Ronald Reagan was president of the United States. He used to be a movie star. So he brought some glamour to the White House.

In fact, glamour was a theme during this decade. People became hooked on TV shows that portrayed glamorous characters. Two of the most popular shows were *Dallas* and *Dynasty*. They were prime-time soap operas. They had the same kind of continuing story line as a daytime soap opera but were on at night.

Dallas and *Dynasty* were shown on the main network channels. Back then, cable television wasn't as big as it is today. It was just getting started. Cable channel owners were experimenting with new types of shows. There was one experiment that proved to be very successful.

You know it as the channel MTV. It was the first nationally available cable network dedicated to music.

Game playing was also popular. It wasn't just limited to children, either. Two really different kinds of games and toys came out during the 1980s. These were Rubik's Cube and Trivial Pursuit. They may have first appeared back then, but they are still challenging gamers today.

But it was not all fun and games during the 1980s. There was also social awareness. People joined together for causes in the United States and worldwide. In 1985, the Live Aid concert featured many famous performers, with the goal to send food to the poor country of Ethiopia in Africa. The following year, Hands Across America raised funds for hunger and homelessness.

Holding "Hands Across America"

On Sunday, May 25, 1986, more than 5 million people held hands. The line of people stretched for 4,152 miles. It went from New York's Battery Park to Long Beach, California. There were some gaps, filled in by miles of red and blue ribbon and some boats. Ultimately the goal was to raise money to fight hunger and homelessness.

People of all ages, races, and faiths participated. Little Leaguers, scout troops, disabled Americans, church groups, and many celebrities were among them. Even President Ronald Reagan and the White House staff were part of it.

Madonna performs at the Live Aid concert on July 13, 1985.

They held hands for about fifteen minutes, starting at 3:00 P.M. EST. They sang patriotic songs, such as "America the Beautiful."

It is not certain how much was raised by the event. But it brought Americans together for a worthwhile cause.

Watching Music? The Birth of MTV

It is hard to imagine a world without music videos. But they were just starting in the 1980s. In fact, MTV did not even go on air until 1981.

Back then, it was a bold idea to devote a channel to music. Warner-Amex Cable took the chance. They asked record companies for free music videos. At the beginning, there were just a couple hundred that they played over and over. But the selection grew, and viewers were hooked.

By 1983, MTV was being seen by 13 million households. The channel continues to be popular today.

The Prime-time Soaps: *Dallas* and *Dynasty*

"Who shot J.R.?" That was the question on the minds of millions of people in 1980. The TV show was called *Dallas*, and it was the ongoing story of the wealthy Ewing family. Greedy J. R. Ewing was shot in the last episode of 1980. Everyone seemed to have a reason to kill him. *Dallas* was one of the most popular TV shows in America during the 1980s. It was also seen all over the world.

(Left to right) Joan Collins as Alexis Carrington, John Forsythe as Blake Carrington, and Linda Evans as Krystle Carrington in *Dynasty*. The characters were fun to watch, but very few people could afford to imitate their upscale style!

Dynasty was another extremely popular prime-time soap opera. The plot centered on the wealthy Carrington family. People watched it for the drama. They also enjoyed the fashions. Actress Joan Collins, who played Alexis Carrington, was watched as much for what she would wear as for the next nasty thing she would do.

Trivial Pursuit and Rubik's Cube

The 1980s had plenty of fun and games. Among these were Trivial Pursuit and the Rubik's Cube. Trivial Pursuit was a game created in 1979 by two Canadians, Scott Abbott and Chris Haney. The players had to answer trivia questions in different categories. By 1984, they were selling 20 million copies in the United States alone.

The Rubik's Cube was created by Hungarian inventor Erno Rubik. The toy was made up of small blocks. Each side of the large cube was a different color. Gamers moved the blocks around to mix up the colors. Then they tried to make each side of the cube a solid color again. It became a huge hit in the early 1980s. But by 1983, the cube was no longer in production. It did come back in the 1990s and is still around today.

A teenager tries to solve the Rubik's Cube. Do you think you can figure it out in record time?

Royal Style

When nineteen-year-old nursery-school assistant Lady Diana Spencer caught the eye of Great Britain's Prince Charles, it was like a fairy tale. Their wedding in 1981 was broadcast worldwide.

Starting with the romantic, puff-sleeved wedding gown, Lady Diana's style was copied again and again. Her frilly high-necked blouses, well-cut suits, slim sheath dresses, and low pumps were popular in everyday dress. Her evening wear was elegant and stylish, often created by top designers.

In the mid-eighties, her marriage fell apart. But because she was mother to the second and third in line for the throne, sons Will and Harry, Diana was considered part of the royal family. She continued to be a fashion icon for women around the world until her tragic death in a car accident at age thirty-six.

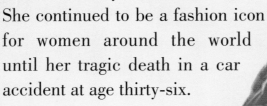

Talk about big fashion in the eighties! Princess Diana's wedding dress had huge puffy sleeves, layers of frills at the neckline, and a twenty-five-foot-long train!

Timeline

The 1920s

The look: cloche hats, dropped-waist dresses, long strands of pearls (women), and baggy pants (men)

The hair: short bobs

The fad: raccoon coats

The 1930s

The look: dropped hemlines, natural waists, practical shoes (women), and blazers and trousers (men)

The hair: finger waves and permanents

The fad: sunbathing

The 1940s

The look: shirtwaist dresses and military style (women) and suits and fedoras (men)

The hair: victory rolls and updos

The fad: kangaroo cloaks

The 1950s

The look: circular skirts and saddle shoes (women) and the greaser look (men)

The hair: bouffants and pompadours

The fad: coonskin caps

The 1960s

The look: bell-bottoms and miniskirts (women) and turtlenecks and hipster pants (men)

The hair: beehives and pageboys

The fad: go-go boots

The 1970s

The look: designer jeans (women) and leisure suits (men)

The hair: shags and Afros

The fad: hot pants

The 1980s

The look: preppy (women and men) and *Miami Vice* (men)

The hair: side ponytails and mullets

The fad: ripped off-the-shoulder sweatshirts

The 1990s

The look: low-rise, straight-leg jeans (both women and men)

The hair: the "Rachel" cut from *Friends*

The fad: ripped, acid-washed jeans

The 2000s

The look: leggings and long tunic tops (women) and the sophisticated urban look (men)

The hair: feminine, face-framing cuts (with straight hair dominating over curly)

The fad: organic and bamboo clothing

Glossary

accessories—Items that are not part of your main clothing but worn with it, such as jewelry, gloves, hats, and belts.

argyle—A knitted pattern of diamonds.

asymmetrical—Uneven.

aviator—A pilot; a style of sunglasses with large lenses usually worn by pilots.

blunt—Straight across.

brooch—A large decorative pin.

dramatic—Theatrical, easily noticed.

executive—Someone who works in a management position.

fad—A craze that happens for a brief period of time.

fashion—The current style of dressing.

frilly—Decorated with ruffles.

icon—A person who represents the characteristics of a group or time period.

Lycra—The brand name for a type of spandex.

monogrammed—A design made up of letters that represent a person's name.

mullet—A haircut that is short in the front and long in the back.

preppy—The fashion worn by students of preparatory school.

scrunchie—An elastic hair tie that is covered in fabric.

tailored—Custom made to fit the body.

trend—The general direction in which things are heading.

yuppie—The nickname for the young urban or upwardly mobile professional.

Further Reading

Books

Carnegy, Vicky. *Fashions of a Decade: The 1980s.* New York: Holiday House, 2007.

Jones, Jen. *Fashion History: Looking Great Through the Ages.* Mankato, Minn.: Capstone Press, 2007.

Leventon, Melissa. *What People Wore When: A Complete Illustrated History of Costume From Ancient Times to the Nineteenth Century for Every Level of Society.* New York: St. Martin's Griffin, 2008.

Steer, Deirdre Clancy. *The 1980s and 1990s.* New York: Chelsea House, 2009.

Internet Addresses

Fashion-Era, "Power Dressing: 1980s Fashion History"
<http://www.fashion-era.com/power_dressing.htm>

Eighty-Eightynine, "80s Culture"
<http://www.eightyeightynine.com/culture/index.html>

Index